The Empath and the Archetypal Drama Triangle

Elaine La Joie

DEDICATION

To Grant, without your love and support, these books would have never been written

CONTENTS

ACKNOWLEDGMENTS

These books are based on combinations of client stories from my private practice and from my own personal experience. There would be no lessons to share with you without the courageous efforts of my clients in healing themselves so they can have the lives and relationships that they desire.

1 INTRODUCTION

I am an Empath who has been working as a coach, mentor, and shaman for about ten years. Most of my clients are also Empaths. I decided to write this series of books when I realized that I repeated the same concepts and materials to my clients, and those clients usually used their new knowledge for great improvement in their lives. Since Empaths tend to love books on self-improvement, writing one of my own seemed like the next right step, especially since not all Empaths have access to their own personal shaman. My teachers have included other Empaths, like Sonia Choquette and Julia Cameron, plus shaman teachers like Alberto Villoldo, Linda Fitch, Debra Grace, Greta Holmes, and Marv Harwood. If you've enjoyed Sonia Choquette's and Julia Cameron's work, you will most likely find these books useful. The shaman likes to get to the deep, nitty-gritty, and sometimes painfully messy work and release it. So, some of the work in this book may not feel inspirational or particularly easy to read. But, if you are an Empath, you probably aren't afraid of dealing with the darker emotional states, and in fact you may be relieved to hear how one Empath overcame obstacles particular to Empaths.

Empaths have the ability to feel the emotions and physical sensations of others, especially our loved ones. In extreme cases, Empaths can develop the same personality traits and physical symptoms of the people to whom they are closest. This ability in the Empath is usually unconscious and therefore uncontrolled. More than anything, Empaths want to have close, loving, bonded, rewarding relationships, and most Empaths want this with a Life

1

Partner. But for many Empaths, the area of Relationship is either difficult or dissatisfying, precisely because we tend to tune in to what the other person needs and then lose ourselves in the process—in other words, we lose that relationship with ourselves as we relate to others. As we come into right relationship with ourselves, old ways of being that did not fit our true selves fall away. Relationships centered around old roles and rules either end or evolve, and new relationships based on our rediscovered selves take their place.

While our goal may be to create wonderful relationships, this journey of healing enough to be ready for such connections can make us wish we had never started the process. It is my hope that by following the stories of typical Empaths in creating the lives that they really wanted, this book will serve as a guide for Empaths who want to understand their relationships and their own hidden motivations. The personal healing work involved can be intense, but it is worth it. May this book help you on your own personal journey.

WHAT IS AN EMPATH?

One way of describing an Empath is the ability of someone to feel the emotional, mental, and physical symptoms of people around the Empath, especially those that the Empath loves, as if those emotions and sensations originated in the Empath. The untrained Empath literally cannot tell the difference between her emotions, thoughts, and physical sensations and those of another. An Empath can easily absorb the emotions of others, and in some cases, she can be overtaken by the physical symptoms of others. Without skill, the Empath can become very ill. Some Empaths are so sensitive that they cannot take public transportation and must avoid large groups of people or feel completely overwhelmed by what most people consider normal stimuli.

Honoring the Empath's sensitivity is the first step in healing. This very sensitivity is the reason that Empaths make natural healers, artists, and intuitives. Empaths can also make great performers, literally channeling their roles. It is this ability to role-play and to respond that can get Empaths into trouble in their relationships; Empaths can confuse a performance or a role with their essential selves.

In such cases Empaths can use their sensitivity to collude with the group instead of honor their individuality. The Empath can be easily caught up in drama because she is so psychically in tune with everyone around her. The ability of the Empath to enmesh herself with others can lead the Empath to waste her life supporting others without her understanding how she became the anchor for their emotional support.

The core trait of the Empath is that he or she is acutely aware of and overly responsive to the emotional needs of others, even if the required response is a rejection. The Empath is unconsciously accommodating. As we will see with the Drama Triangle the expected responses change invariably from friendly gestures into attacks, which can be horribly confusing for Empaths. In other words, the Empath tends to react instead of choose a response consciously. How do we catch a glimpse of the overarching dynamic when we as Empaths are stuck in the emotional realm?

THE MYTHIC REALITY: ARCHETYPES

My discussion of the Empath, especially within relationships, hinges on understanding the archetypal nature of the human experience. Archetypes are forces that are common to all human beings—they are part of the collective consciousness. The Empath can be described as an archetype. When we understand ourselves as archetype, we can understand our behavior in a less personalized way. Knowing the other archetypes with which Empaths tend to interact also helps us understand our relationships and how those predictably will unfold. In future ebooks I will discuss the Empath as an Enneagram Archetype, the Type Four, in more detail. However, in this book I'll concentrate on the archetypal nature of the Drama Triangle of Disempowerment, with its archetypes of Victim, Rescuer, and Bully.

Empaths, because we are so responsive, and because we usually have been victimized in childhood, tend to get caught on the Drama Triangle. I have found in my practice that understanding the Drama Triangle and the Empath as archetype are extremely helpful for my clients in living a life free of the pitfalls of these archetypal forces. An Empath stuck on the Drama Triangle tends to live a life full of regrets and resentment while being perpetually drained of energy, unable to fulfill her craving for a creative life. An Empath who can recognize an invitation to enter the Drama Triangle is an Empath who can choose to channel her energy in positive, creative ways rather than wasting her life force.

THE MYTHIC REALITY: SHAMANIC WORK AND THE SACRED

Let me introduce the concept of the four different but nested layers of reality that the shaman recognizes so you will have the same perspective and terminology as my clients. In western society we are very familiar with the Literal Level, which includes the physical realm. Surrounding the physical body is the second level, the Symbolic, which includes the mental mind of words and emotions. In western society we tend to divide the mental mind and the emotions into two separate bodies, but from the shamanic perspective they are both in the Symbolic realm. Most counseling and therapy happens at the Symbolic level, the realm of language. Surrounding the Symbolic level is the Mythic level, which includes the Imagination and Archetypes but does not contain words. Surrounding the Mythic level is the Energetic level, which includes the aura, the meridians, and the chakra system. As a shaman, I work with all four levels, but mostly I work at the Mythic and Energetic levels with my clients.

Teaching my clients to move into the Sacred, or the Mythic level can bring lasting change for many Empaths, who tend to create problems for themselves on the Emotional level. If you are reading this book, you probably are an Empath that hasn't had much success solving problems at the Symbolic level (mental mind and emotions); you might have become sick at the Literal level (the physical body) with various chronic physical ailments. Stepping into the Mythic plane and understanding archetypal forces may help ease suffering that in many cases is unnecessary.

When we step into the Mythic realm, we are stepping into an overview of the situation at hand. From the Mythic level we discover that archetypal forces run more of our literal lives than we realize. This also means that by understanding the archetypal nature of relationships, we can apply knowledge of the archetypes, especially those on the Drama Triangle, to many situations at the Literal and Symbolic levels of our lives.

On the Literal level nothing much may look amiss when a friend who is only five years younger than us tells us he thinks of us as his Big Sis. On the Symbolic level as Empaths we may get a weird vibe but reason with ourselves that we should feel honored to be thought of as Family. But by looking from the Mythic level we may see that our friend is trapped in the Victim Role as the Improperly Mothered Child and is projecting his old wounds onto us—we feel weird because we are expected to Mother him—we've been placed in the Role of Rescuer because his power to feel good about himself has been given over to us, and we may not be interested in playing that role. At the Energetic level we may see cords from our friend to us that pinch, bind and even drain us of our energy.

At the Mythic level, we can learn that most of Life is not personal (and Empaths tend to take everything personally.) Knowing that not much is personal can give us freedom to choose to engage or not to engage a relationship or a situation and therefore make it personal to us. Life becomes a practice of self-mastery instead of simply unconsciously living out a few archetypal forces. Life also becomes more fun, joyful, and somewhat funny as we live from the realm of the Sacred. Empaths tend to be serious, so learning to live from the Mythic helps us not take our moods or our problems quite so seriously.

In modern Western Society, we have left much of the honoring of the Mythic experience behind. The Mythic level is not only the place of the archetypes, but it is also the realm of the Soul or the Heart. When we leave this reality out of our lives, Empaths tend to become disconnected from our hearts and stuck in the Emotional/Mental realm. If problems arise at the Emotional/Mental realm, then Empaths can become physically ill as well as we try to process this heavy energy through the physical body. When the Empath learns how to live consciously from the Mythic level, problems at the Emotional plane can be solved at the Mythic plane instead of processed at the Physical plane. Since the Mythic plane of consciousness does not have a "mental mind" it can be hard for us Westerners to figure out how it works enough to trust that it does work. If we don't know how it works, we might tend to dismiss it as silly. Instead of trying to figure out the Mythic realm, in this book I'll go straight to my personal experience and those of my clients to show the changes that can happen when we treat our entire life as Sacred by living from the Mythic level. When we can see our lives from the universal instead of the personal, the Empath suddenly has more choice and more freedom.

Let's look at one of the most powerful Archetypal forces in the human realm, the Drama Triangle of Disempowerment. Every human being has played on the Drama Triangle. Empaths are extremely prone to falling prey to Drama because we are so responsive, and because we are unconsciously looking for clues of what to do next in relation to others. Being at choice on whether to enter into a Drama means that most of the time we will not choose drama, we'll instead choose something more creative. We have more energy to explore the gifts of the Empath: the ability to form deep connections and to enjoy extraordinary creativity. In turn, the Empath brings gifts to the rest of humanity in the form of healthy relationships, supportive community, and inspiring works of art.

2 THE DRAMA TRIANGLE OF DISEMPOWERMENT

When a client is having trouble with a relationship, we always discuss the Drama Triangle of Disempowerment. Understanding the Drama Triangle requires no knowledge of psychology or shamanic interventions. The Drama Triangle is simple to understand. When we know how it works, we can take a step back and observe our behavior in a Drama Triangle situation. We can choose to do something more creative than what the Drama Triangle draws out of us.

As stated in the Introduction, the Drama Triangle of Disempowerment is an archetypal phenomenon, which means it influences all human beings as individuals and as groups. The Drama Triangle is interesting because it is dynamic—a person caught on the Triangle alternates amongst roles as a Drama plays itself out, and the force of the roles is strong because of its collective nature. What this means is that we can be caught in Drama and be totally conscious of it, but still find ourselves pulled into Rescuer or Bully or Victim behavior. Staying out of Drama is a practice. Understanding our own personal ways of engaging in Drama can help us recognize the invitations from others to play. For Empaths, having a choice whether to engage is usually a new concept; we react instead.

Drama Triangle Basics

The Drama Triangle consists of three Archetypal Roles: Victim,

Rescuer, and Perpetrator or Bully. We have all seen ourselves as Victims at one time or another. And, some of us truly have been victimized. However, it is the attachment to the Role of Victim that creates the potential for Drama. Most of us have chosen to rescue another, and there are healthy ways to rescue, such as a firefighter saving the child from a burning building. However, when we are attached to the Role of Rescuer, we usually engage a Victim that is also attached to being victimized. This sets up two sides of the Drama Triangle. The third position is the Perpetrator, or Bully. We have all acted as Bullies, and this role is not pleasant to look at in ourselves. Traditional Bullies go looking for a weakling to victimize in order to make themselves feel strong. As Drama plays out, Victims become Bullies when a Rescuer doesn't fulfill his role, or Rescuers can become Bullies to rescue Victims.

Each role holds a Vibration that attracts its complement
Victim and Bully, Classic

Being a Victim always invites either a Rescuer or a Bully. This happens energetically whether we consciously intend it or not, or whether the person that is pulled in is normally a Rescuer or a Perpetrator. An example of this vibration pull happened while I was coaching one of my first clients, a friend of more than twenty years that I loved dearly. She was immersed in the story of how she had been victimized by male authority figures over and over during her college years.

What startled me is that the more I listened to her story, and the more entrenched she was in how she had been victimized, the more the urge to verbally abuse her was pulled out of me. I literally wanted to shout at her the same abuse these other people had used against her. It was an energetic effect of her field pulling the response to her—she was literally attracting a Perpetrator. I, of course, did not verbally abuse her, but it did strike home the power of our field in each moment, and how it attracts to us what we want and do not want. If I had abused her, I would have stepped into the Bully role. However, being pulled in because of the vibration of the Victim energy would NOT have excused my Bully behavior. And, once again, my friend was not asking nor deserved to be abused.

Another example of this phenomenon happened to another

client of mine, the gentlest, heart-centered man I have ever met. He was walking down the hall, observing a fearful woman coming from the opposite direction. She kept her head down, but furtively looked over her shoulder, trying to keep herself safe. She accidentally bumped into my client. Her look of fear and her cringing pulled the urge out of him to strike her. He was horrified, and would never do such a thing, but the vibration of being a Victim usually does pull in a vibration of Bully. If we are not careful, we can find ourselves behaving in ways that we would never consider just because the other person is holding a certain vibe or role. This is especially important for Empaths to be aware of, since as Empaths we respond to another's emotional vibration without thinking.

Victim and Rescuer, Classic

The other role Victim energy pulls in is a Rescuer. The traditional romantic archetype of the Princess and the White Knight is one which most of us learned in childhood. The princess usually has been victimized in some way and the knight comes in to rescue her from a situation or Bully. Most Empaths have a strong fantasy in which they are this type of Victim, and they are waiting for this type of Rescue. Many Rescuers find their meaning in life in being caretakers for life long Victims. However, when the Victim starts to heal herself, the Rescuer can feel threatened that he is no longer needed and can actively engage in keeping the Victim helpless and powerless. But what we don't realize can happen is that we can play all three roles with the same people involved. If the Victim doesn't like the way her Rescuer is rescuing her, she can suddenly turn into a Bully, demanding that the Rescuer take care of her and blaming him for her state. The Rescuer in turn will feel trapped and victimized.

Another Classic Victim and Rescuer Drama can occur between adults, but one person takes up a child role (Victim) and the other person takes up a parent role. (Rescuer) People with severe unhealed parental wounds tend to create a string of broken relationships with others who are the same sex as the faulty parent. In other words, men who have unhealed mother wounds tend to create poor relationships with women, or women with unhealed mother wounds tend to create poor relationships with other women. This scenario is especially pertinent for Empaths, who, once they've addressed their tendency to be Victims, are usually seen as competent and nurturing. We will go over examples of how this wound tends to play out, since it is the most common Drama I have dealt with in my practice.

Three person Triangle, Easing Tension between Victim and Rescuer

If tension grows between a Victim and Rescuer but it is too threatening for the couple to handle, they can pull in a third person to fill the other role and disperse the tension between them but the third person pays for it by both people in the couple turning into Bullies and turning on the third person. I unwittingly entered this type dynamic when I was first a student of shamanic work. The husband of a firmly entrenched Victim called me, wanting soul retrieval work done for his wife. He was intent on fixing her. The wife met with me several times, and as she gained her power back, she admitted that her husband's Rescuing was smothering her, and that if she did heal she was going to have to leave him. What I missed seeing was that I had now taken over the role of Rescuer for her so she could admit her husband was a Bully. Everything she hated about her husband came pouring out of her. With me in the Rescuer position, she had the strength to leave him. The husband began undermining the soul retrieval work, claiming that it was creating distance between them. He started to become scary—he was becoming a Bully—in order to maintain the status quo. When I saw this behavior unfolding, I became afraid for my safety and for hers, and asked her to engage other help. She then turned on me for a failed Rescue and went back to her husband. I was now the Bully for not Rescuing her the way she wanted. It was much safer for her to go from Victim to Bully and lash out at me rather than at her husband.

In fact, the couple was in a very stable dynamic of his Rescuing her, but her feeling Victimized by his Bullying Rescue, and so they attract in a new Rescuer. The new Rescuer is seen as a wonderful help at first. But, as the Victim starts to heal, the original Rescuer's purpose in life is threatened. The original Rescuer begins to feel powerless and even Victimized by his wife's healing. The new Rescuer is to blame for this. By turning into an overt Bully, he frightens away the new Rescuer. The Victim, feeling abandoned yet again, turns Bully and Victimizes the new Rescuer. Then she goes back to her original Rescuer, sure that no one can help her and no one is trustworthy but him, reinforcing her Victimhood. If I had been paying attention, I would have heard the stories of other incompetent healers (Rescuers) who had failed them in the past, and would have expected to be placed on the bone pile, too.

The Empath caught in another person's Drama

Perhaps the most confusing Drama is to be caught in someone else's Drama, and to discover ourselves playing out a role that has nothing to do with our essential selves. Empaths are easily caught up in other people's Dramas because we are so psychically in tune with everyone around us. We know unconsciously exactly what roles to take up and play. For most Empaths, learning how to spot an invitation to enter Drama and then choosing not to engage is essential to living a truly authentic life. I have seen Empaths go along for years in someone else's Drama, fulfilling someone else's agenda, and then suddenly wake up, wondering how they could have behaved that way in the first place.

This sort of collusion can have terrible consequences for all involved. For the Empath, she has taken on a role that she might not have chosen consciously for herself. She can find that her relationship with the other has been unreal or full of pretense. Since the classic Empath prides herself on being authentic, finding that she has colluded with another person's Drama or Illusion can feel humiliating and confusing. The Empath can believe that she has no right to leave the Drama—the role can feel like a non-negotiable contract for many Empaths.

The Drama Triangle is emotionally and physically draining. This is energy that could be used instead for our creative endeavors. When we fall into other people's Dramas, Empaths can feel trapped, out of control, and confused. We can fixate on what happened within the Drama when the way out of confusion is to get off the Triangle completely. As Empaths we have a hard time letting a confusing situation go because we want to fix it or at least understand it. However, our tendency to want to make the situation better only leads to more Drama, since Drama can never be fixed, as we will see.

The Empath creates Drama as an effective self-sabotage

Unhealthy Empaths tend to use Drama to keep emotions at a height as a great form of self-sabotage. Some Empaths can start a Drama just to avoid dealing with their creativity or a relationship that must change. Once again, an Empath stuck in Drama is an Empath who is wasting her life force. If we are too tired to address what really needs fixing, then we can avoid changing our lives. If we find ourselves with the urge to create Drama, the better question to ask ourselves is, "What am I trying to avoid creating?" or "What do I know needs to change but I'd rather not face it just yet?" Instigating Drama can serve as a well-orchestrated temper tantrum.

If neither question yields an obvious answer, sometimes when an Empath creates Drama, and she takes up the Victim position, it can mean that we have an old wound that needs addressing and healing, but we aren't fully conscious of the problem. We act it out through Drama, expecting a Rescue or a Bullying, or both, depending on the original wound. This is the perfect opportunity to visit a shaman for soul retrieval work, discussed throughout these books.

The Conscious Empath

Understanding how to separate her actions from those of a Drama can help to make sense of situations in which she has given her power over to the system instead of living her own life. Understanding the typical behavior of people engaged in Drama is also helpful. But, understanding her own propensity to create Drama is the most powerful tool to staying out of and not being hooked by invitations to waste time and energy on the Drama Triangle. It's important to remember that even though the Drama Triangle is an Archetypal phenomenon and as such it can "pull" behavior out of us, each of us, no matter where we are on the Triangle, is always responsible for our part in the Drama, and certainly our actions. In other words, it is completely inexcusable for a Bully to justify her Bully behavior because the Victim's vibration "made her do it." The whole point is to become responsible, empowered human beings, at choice about our behavior.

As we move forward in these examples, we'll also see that each

Archetype Role has a set of assumptions or beliefs about itself and the other positions on the triangle. If we tend to have those beliefs separate from the archetype, we will tend to play one role more strongly or commonly when we fall into Drama. As an example, most Empaths have beliefs around feeling trapped, rejected, abandoned, or having little influence in the world. As such, it is easy to fall into the Role of Victim.

Empath as Victim

For many unhealed Empaths, Drama is a safe space from which to live. It is a great distraction to becoming whole, and it gives a purpose and meaning to life, even if it isn't a life lived from the Soul. Unhealthy Empaths tend to take up the Victim Role because of trauma in their childhoods. Many times we have been true victims. But what tends to happen if the Empath does not heal the wound is that she takes up the archetypal role of Victim. Then she has a hard time leading an empowered life. She may expect someone to Rescue her, like the White Knight or Prince Charming mentioned above. Many times that White Knight turns into a Bully and the Empath is further traumatized. When others do not collude with her Victim position, she can turn Bully and attack them for being unsupportive. Or, the Empath can interpret everything from her Victim role, even though others may not intend to Victimize her. She can carry the vibration of Victim with her, inviting attacks and rescues, but not understanding how she is attracting these Dramas to her.

Emerging from the role of Victim is frightening because it entails taking full responsibility for our lives. While we are not responsible for being victims of childhood traumas, what we are responsible for is healing those wounds, getting help with our patterns and beliefs, and doing the work so we don't have to live as Victims any longer and perpetuate the Drama Triangle to our other relationships. Taking full responsibility for our lives is very scary, but a commitment to do so one step at a time is the first step needed. These baby steps mean that we will steadily heal and get better. We must be gentle with ourselves as we go through the process, but also firm, willing to catch ourselves assigning blame to others or to ourselves.

Empath as Rescuer

Once the Empath does her work of dealing with the Role of Victim, then she usually moves on to understanding how she plays Rescuer. Empaths tend to Rescue others by being the emotional processor for family and friends. This can be done while being a Victim as well, but many Empaths pride themselves on how necessary they are to their friends and family—a sure sign of Rescuer behavior. Empaths tend to be the ones that others confide in. In fact, they can get into trouble by being the only one someone confides in, as we will see later in the Secret Drama essay in the Family System section. Empaths also tend to focus on what needs fixing, so they can usually see how to solve the other person's problems. The trouble with the Rescuer Role is that it takes away personal power from the Victim, or whoever is being Rescued. And usually Rescuers expect a return on their investment like the Giving Persona. (See the Motivations of the Empath ebook for a fuller description of the Giving Persona, a type of Empath) Also, Rescuers feel obligated towards their Victims. A Victim may demand that the Rescuer fulfill the role, and even though the Rescuer may not want to, she will tend to feel like she owes it to the Victim and feel huge guilt for refusing. Empath's must learn not to believe it when another tells the Empath how necessary the Empath is to this other person's life. The Empath must strive to make all her adult relationships equal, with each person responsible for her life and choices. Once the Empath stops believing in the Noble Rescuer Role and stops taking power away (or at least accepting power) from the Victim, then she's in a new position of acting as a Coach rather than a Rescuer. A Coach helps others step into their personal power by giving support and encouragement, rather than fixing the situation to save or help the Victim.

Empath as Bully

Empaths fall into the Perpetrator or Bully role when they feel forced to defend themselves from attack. Because Empaths are usually highly sensitive not to just emotional energy but also to stimulation in general, they become overwhelmed more quickly than most people. If someone isn't aware of the Empath's sensitivity, he can overwhelm the Empath, and in return, the Empath can attack the other person, even though no malice was intended. This unfortunate occurrence usually leads to the Empath being attacked in return.

Empaths sometimes need to use anger and aggression to hold firm, especially when they've been trained in life not to give a clear No to others who want something from them that they do not want to give. If Empaths aren't careful, they can slip straight into the Bully role and begin feeling contempt towards whoever has violated their boundaries. Once negative thoughts attach to the feelings of contempt, the relationship takes a hateful spin for the Empath, and usually cannot be salvaged.

Another instance of common Empath Bully behavior can be triggered by being disappointed in someone the Empath admires or has put on a pedestal. In this case, the Empath is first in the Victim position looking for a Rescuer. When the Rescue fails, as it always does, the Empath can be so disillusioned she attacks the Failed Rescuer with contempt and hatred. We'll look deeper at this when we look at the essay on the Mother Wound and Putting Others on a Pedestal discussed in the Shadow Work ebook.

Empath off the Drama Triangle

As the Empath comes to understand how she plays all three roles of Drama, she can be vigilant in not taking up those roles. With practice she stays out of Drama and has energy that was wasted in Drama available for Creativity and a fulfilled life. Staying out of Drama is a practice, but eventually the healthy Empath masters this. The added benefit of being off the Drama Triangle is that it offers protection from relationships and energetic cording that usually drain the Empath. In fact, learning to not accept invitations to enter Drama, and quietly refusing to engage in Drama is the best energetic protection for Empaths because their emotional energy stays conserved.

The following essays are examples of Drama in which Empaths tend to engage. If you see yourself in any of these essays, just take it as an indication that more practice at staying out of Drama is needed, and begin practicing! If the pattern is hard to move, then please take the issue to a shaman—soul retrieval work (discussed in the

Shamanic Energy Work ebook) can be very helpful in moving stuck beliefs that lead to emotional pain and unhappy outcomes. Already we've seen that the Classic Empath tends to fall into the Victim role, and the Giving Persona tends to fall into the Rescuer role. One Drama can go on for years with different individuals stepping in to play the roles. It can also be played collectively between groups or nations. The following essays are a few examples of Drama in action with at least one Empath involved. Most of these examples come from my practice, and most of my clients are Classic Empaths. As Classic Empaths we usually prefer to start in the Victim position. However, as we will see shortly, Empaths will turn into Rescuers and Justified Bullies perhaps more easily than the average person because we are so in tune with whatever is happening on the emotional plane. We will fall into whatever role is required by the Drama. If we can understand Drama and the typical permutations of Drama, we can be at choice whether to engage.

3 THE UNDERDOG VICTIM

There's a type of Victim who feeds off the energy of others, but the way she ensnares another is by pretending to walk a conscious spiritual path. Since a spiritual walk includes interdependence, she asks for help and support, usually from nice people who aren't self-assertive. Naturally, the people whom she asks for help want to be supportive. Once she has supporters, instead of empowering herself with their assistance, she uses their connection as a food source and maintains it with guilt tripping. These are people who say, "I've been told by our spiritual guru that I'm supposed to ask for support, so can I stay with you while I'm looking for an apartment?" even though you just told them that you were so looking forward to spending some quality time with a spouse or a friend that weekend. If the supporter says no, not only is she not helping the Victim, but she's going against what the guru recommended, too. If she says yes, she makes it clear to the Victim that the Victim is more important than the supporter's own needs and falls into the Rescuer trap.

These big-time Victims like to see themselves as Underdogs trying to do the right thing under difficult and scary circumstances. As such, they feel like they have the right to complain to anyone who will listen: their lives are so hard, they are putting in so much effort to surmount their challenges, but the environment around them is so draining. They join spiritual groups, honestly invested in improving themselves but wanting to keep their right to be weak and therefore not responsible for what manifests in their lives. They want guarantees that they will be rewarded with success when they are unwilling to take risks that make success possible. They become angry when they learn that risk means a chance for failure, and that is just part of the game of Life.

These people are so entrenched in Victim that encouragement and belief in their strength can lead them to attack their supporters as being unsupportive. When it is pointed out to them that a colleague in similar circumstances accomplished a similar goal as a way of encouraging the Victim and letting her know all can be well, the Victim will point out all the ways she is different from the successful person. She doesn't have the nurturing family that that person had. Or she doesn't have the financial resources. Or she doesn't have the friends and connections. Or she doesn't have the raw talent. Or she is too young, old, whatever. She will come up with some excuse for why she is an automatic failure and cannot put forth the effort. However, she sees herself as someone right on the verge of success if only the conditions were right, but conditions are never right. When a supporter tells her, if I can do it, you can do it, she complains instead that she is being made to feel that her efforts aren't good enough, since she hasn't yet done it. What she wants reinforced is how weak she is, so she doesn't have to do what others do, and so naturally she needs more help and support. The rules of personal empowerment do not apply to her.

If one of her supporters is gaining success and manifesting her dreams, especially after a path of uncertainty and challenge, the Victim is sure to look for the right moment to sabotage her. The Victim can't stand evidence that personal empowerment and risk taking are the key to success, so she is very good at stabbing those who succeed in the back energetically to set them off balance. She will pick a time to air grievances when her supporter is concentrating on others things besides her, such as the day before a wedding, or right after a friend has given birth. Energetically the supporter is vulnerable; stirring up more emotional conflict at such times gives the Victim a great energetic feeding. Eventually her supporters have enough of such behavior and leave.

Those supporters that remain feel guilty for wanting to abandon the Victim, but they also feel resentful that the support the Victim takes is more than they planned on giving. At this point the Victim senses that her supporters aren't comfortable with her but are unwilling to say so. The Victim cannot stand to hear the truth that she is a big whiner, so she defensively whines some more in an effort to garner more sympathy or at least create more guilt for her Victim state. Then her supporters would really be Bullies if they spoke up.

Not wanting to engage her or feel like a Bully, her supporters avoid setting boundaries with her. The Victim knows that she needs to use others for all she can first; avoiding an honest conversation stretches out the time she is connected to and draining her supporters. When it becomes clear she has lost support, she can righteously blow up at those burned out Rescuers for being mean and withholding. In this way she can blame the drained supporter for her latest setback instead of look closely at herself.

Interestingly enough, this type of person complains that others are draining the life force out of her! And, if we stick around to listen to her story, we will hear how she stayed in the job that drained her for several years, how she put up with a controlling boss, how she involved herself with a married man who had no intention of leaving his wife, how she had friends she couldn't tell to leave her alone because they were Vampires. On top of this, she did so and so for them, and she got no return for it.

To avoid such Victims in the first place, it is important to look at how we tend to be Rescuers. Are we willing to do more in the relationship than the other person? Do we attach importance or spiritual goodness to being supportive and loving? If so, we are perfect matches for such Victims. Giving up the role of Rescuer is the way not to attract such a Victim. Recognizing this type of Victim behavior becomes easier once the Rescuer role is set aside.

If we have unwittingly entered such a relationship, the way out is to be clear and act on our vibes and speak up when conflict with the Victim comes up. This doesn't mean that we have to be confrontational, but with the people who are important to us, and who have close relationships with us, or who would like to believe that they do and we are behaving as if they do, it's important to be clear. Speaking up and setting boundaries will have the cost of the Victim turning Bully for the failure of a continued Rescue, but the damage with such people is usually temporary as they soon turn their energy to attaching to another Rescuer.

If you recognize yourself as the Victim in this example, the way out of Victimhood is to realize that there is a direct payoff to being a Victim—this Victim does not have to make progress or take risks.

Wanting to release the Victim role and step into self-empowerment is scary. Look closely at where you offer support. Was it asked for? Does the other person reciprocate or acknowledge your efforts? Are they setting limits with you but are you ignoring them? Do you wonder why the other doesn't offer more closeness when that is what you are offering them? Are you afraid of failure and so there's a huge investment in not moving forward but remaining stuck? Are you afraid of risk and so try to arrange circumstances for a guaranteed success? If you've answered yes to all these questions and others have betrayed you or not lived up to your standards of loving support, you probably are an Underdog Victim.

Moving out of this state takes tremendous courage and support. Being firm and disciplined, and offering no excuses for putting in effort are the keys to Underdogs learning how to be whole enough to venture out in the world without having to latch on to others. Sometimes just the admittance of such dependent behavior starts a long term healing process.

4 THE VAMPIRE VICTIM AND THE WEAK RESCUER

The Emotional and Energetic Vampire Victim is so wounded that she is willing to appear in any way required in order to stay connected to her Rescuer. This type of Victim is particularly dangerous to Spiritual Seekers who equate being compassionate and nice for being Spiritually good. Many times this Victim can be unconscious of her behavior, and that unconsciousness becomes an excuse for the Rescuer for staying bound; the Rescuer can't hold her wounded behavior against her because she doesn't know what she is doing. If the Rescuer is not careful, his life force will be drained away in order to keep the Victim whole. The Victim literally is so wounded that she cannot provide an emotionally safe container for herself, so looks for it in another. And if she finds another willing to be connected to her, but then he decides to disconnect, she'll do anything to prevent him from leaving, including behaving as if she has suddenly become whole.

I had a client who was craving a soul mate connection on the physical, emotional, and spiritual levels. He had been married for ten years, but his wife was emotionally unavailable, and even though they were still married, that marriage was effectively dead, but not declared dead. He met a woman at work who was deeply passionate and creative. She was also charming and supported herself by getting people around her to provide her with whatever she needed. A great warning sign for Empaths who are looking for a deep connection is to watch carefully people who use charm to get what they want. That is a clear sign that others are being fooled into doing things for the charmer that they wouldn't normally do because that charmer knows how to make them feel special.

My client was also highly creative, but because he had this missing component of love in his life, this woman spotted him energetically and went after him as a mate. She knew he was married but knew there was no emotional connection left there. To her, he was not only emotionally available, but he also had enough extra life force to provide her a container and help her feel good about herself.

For my client, what he saw was a beautiful, charming woman, full of love for him, who wanted to be with him the way his wife could not. In fact, she was everything his wife was not and she was also a complement to many aspects of his personality. For my client, the feeling of love was so strong, and the idea of being with her and sharing an impassioned, fast-moving lifestyle were very attractive. And yet, he had misgivings that this woman did not share the same spiritual philosophy that he did. He also saw how she was willing to use and manipulate others to get what she wanted.

Each time my client became clear that he needed to break it off with the Victim, she did what she could to keep him bound to her. Her first tactic was to become angry and defensive, hoping that he would apologize and come after her. She even left a belonging or two in his room to leave the reason (and the energetic hook) for him to contact her again.

When that failed to work, she wore him down emotionally and physically by wanting to talk and achieve clarity. Now, this wasn't her just wanting to talk. This was her wanting to talk in bed while naked at three in the morning after being told he needed a break from the sexual relationship. Or, it was her wanting to talk on the way to a work meeting while he was a captive audience. The talk included facts and revelations that were meant to flatter and make the Rescuer feel special. (Attachment to feeling special is a particular trap for Empaths.) The Victim said things such as, "I feel loved and safe only when I'm around you." Or, "You are the only one that I let touch me," or "I've never been able to sleep comfortably next to a man, except you." These comments were designed to make the Rescuer feel as if he was needed personally, when in fact Spirit provides the people, places, and things that we need, if we are not dependent on specifics. The Victim makes things personal as a way of keeping the energetic hooks in.

The Victim also pulls in third parties to make her look like the innocent Victim so that her Rescuer will rescue her from unreasonable Bullies, strengthening the emotional connection. In this case, the wife of my client had the compulsive urge in the middle of the night to call her husband and berate him for cheating on her, even though that was not her style, and even though she had agreed amicably to a separation. This was actually the energetic effect of the Drama Triangle the Victim was counting on. The wife was pulled in energetically to act as a Bully. If the wife blames the Victim, Victimizing her further, the Rescuer feels energetically obligated to protect the Victim's position.

When this Victim sees that she is losing her grip on her Rescuer, she actively recruits other Rescuer/Bullies, using emotional blackmail and threats to show the Rescuer that he is putting her in bad straights. She might tell her Rescuer that so-and-so wants to punch him out, or wants to talk to him, hoping that he'll see that there will be severe consequences if he leaves. Or she will call in other third parties that will step in and excuse the Victim's manipulative behavior, telling the Rescuer, she's going through a hard time right now, but she's really a good person, please ignore her bad behavior. This Victim cannot stand on her own in any circumstances, and is willing to behave badly in order to get her way, and if that doesn't work, in order to punish.

However, the sneakiest thing I've seen these Victims do is use the spiritual philosophy and the claim of revelation and healing to keep the Rescuer bound. When my client made it clear that they were not compatible given their different religious and spiritual views, the day before he was to leave her, she had an in-the-middle-of-the-night epiphany that she wanted to be more open to his philosophy. She even magically produced friends who had his same spiritual bent who hadn't felt comfortable discussing it with her so that he could see that she was open to new ideas, and that she did have in her life the connections that he craved.

Even though she may not be setting this up consciously, and she believes her love is real, the problem is she is going about this with an agenda of keeping my client bound to her. She wants a long term commitment from him, and will do everything she can to keep him emotionally bound, whereas the person who truly is living from Spirit understands that the only real connections we have with others happen when they come freely given with no agendas. We decide that we want to be together, we freely choose it, and it makes us feel good, plus it is always voluntary and temporary and is subject to change and negotiation. That is a healthy relationship.

Instead my client is constantly off balance. Whenever he becomes clear and decides he wants out, she pulls him back and shows him what he needs to see in order to keep him. Ultimately my client will figure this out and will leave her, but in the meantime he is wasting precious time and energy.

Healing for the Vampire Victim comes from realizing that all her motivation in life is to find an emotional container to make her feel good and safe. And that inherently means she must have someone to Rescue her. When the Vampire Victim realizes this about herself, the next step is to refuse to follow the urge to have a Rescuer in her life. She needs to begin the journey of self-empowerment by standing on her own, without any romantic attachments or other attachments. Others must be allowed to freely come and go, with no strings attached.

These Vampire Victims who go through this healing process experience tremendous agony as they relive old woundings of being not only abandoned in childhood, but most likely drained by others around them. Having an emotionally safe container to hold them as they go through these old emotions is essential, either with a therapist or a shaman. However, these Victims must come to their healing on their own, and not at the prompting of their Rescuer. Many of these Vampire Victims go through a healing process as a way of showing their Rescuer they are motivated to change, when really they are only placating their Rescuer.

For my client, the way out of being a Rescuer is to stop playing on the Drama Triangle. Then it is to look at what is missing from his life that allowed him to be seduced in such a way. Next he must look carefully at what it really means to live the free and spirit-based life that he wanted, with no compromises. Part of his confusion stems from believing that the Victim has a beautiful soul, and so he should stick by her, especially since he is in love.

We ALL have beautiful souls. We are all deserving of love and our heart's desires. However, we are all wounded to some degree or another, and those wounds and the confusions that arise out of them

THE EMPATH AND THE ARCHETYPAL DRAMA TRIANGLE

cause behavior patterns that are hurtful. It is self-mastery to not let our wounds get in our way or hurt others. But another part of self-mastery is not letting other's wounds get in our way or hurt us. This type of discernment sees every person's beautiful soul, but allows our soul to shine through without having to heal anyone else in the process.

5 THE GUILT TRIPPING RESCUER

When we live on the Drama Triangle, our lives are confusing and painful. For Empaths, once we understand how we live as Victims and we give up the role, then we can move on to understanding the Rescuer side of the Drama triangle.

Someone who is used to being Rescued will usually guilt trip the Rescuer by saying something like, "How can you do this and make everyone else unhappy?" That person is depending on the Rescuer to rescue him and others from unhappiness. This is especially potent against someone with a Giving Persona. (See Motivations of the Empath ebook for a fuller description of the Giving Persona.) However, when the Rescuer guilt trips, the Rescuer is much more manipulative. The Rescuer helps others while having a hidden agenda. Usually this agenda is unconscious even to them. Without knowing it the Rescuer's agenda usually goes along the lines of, "I am doing this for you, so you owe me forever. If you don't pay me back the way I want, then you have taken advantage of me." Another assumption the Rescuer makes is that the person being Rescued always has less power than the Rescuer. In other words, the Rescuer is needed and necessary.

For someone who is not on the Drama Triangle and is simply interacting with the Rescuer as if all exchanges were equal, voluntary, and final with each exchange, it can be an unpleasant surprise to find that they have been dealing with a Rescuer, especially when it becomes clear to the Rescuer that he isn't needed after all.

I have had this happen to me with clients. Many times I have former clients come to me, asking me if they can pay for sessions for a friend or loved one. In a few cases, it is a Rescuer asking for help for his friend. The classic Rescuer uses strong-arm tactics such as, "You must let me pay for the session because she won't be able to afford the energy work in any other way, and she really needs it." In such cases the Rescuer is depending on my also being a Rescuer or else I might not be moved to help his disempowered friend. This person doesn't realize he is acting inappropriately; he is so entrenched in Rescuing others. In these cases it is easy to remove myself from the invitation to enter the Triangle by telling them how I do third party payments (which is the exchange of money must happen between them, and then the friend can hire me directly.) Then the friend can exercise his power and choose to work with me, with an investment and the sobering experience of money changing hands.

In a more manipulative case, I had a client who loved my work, had referred many people to me, which I greatly appreciated, and had also had several sessions with me. However, when this client's wife missed a session with me with no notice at all and an inadequate excuse, and I held her to my usual terms for missed sessions, my client was enraged. This client told me that I was treating him unfairly because he had done plenty of sessions with me in the past, he had referred many other clients to me, that I was practicing bad business and that he felt burned that I wasn't treating him as a loyal customer. Notice that it is his wife that missed the session, but it is he who complained about it.

The assumption of the Rescuer is that the person in need of help is not as capable as the Rescuer—this means that the Rescuer will step in and interfere without knowing that is what he is doing. Boundaries become confused or non-existent. His wife did not talk to me directly; the Rescuing husband had to instead. And yet, he could not see that he was interfering in the relationship between his wife and me—the Rescuer literally cannot see the boundary between himself and the Victim. He could not see that he was taking power away from his wife by his confronting me instead of her confronting me. Not only that, the Rescuer automatically puts others into roles of Victim and Bully. His immediate assumption was that I was Bullying his wife, and that in turn he must Bully me back. He cannot tell the difference between himself and his Victim, so he feels Victimized as well.

The other assumption, hidden from the Rescuer, is that help has strings attached to it. An obligation is now in place that the other did not necessarily agree to, but the Rescuer expects. From his perspective he had Rescued me and my practice by providing me business, and now I was indebted to him for his getting my practice off the ground. (From my perspective the work we had done stood alone, and while I was happy to have his business and be of service, we had made a clean exchange, and that was that.) In fact, from his perspective there was an expectation that he (and his wife) would not be held to the normal rules of sessions with me because he held a special place as a "good" client. I owed them special treatment, for all time. This person, from his stance as unconscious Rescuer, fell right into the Victim position when his Rescuer strategy failed him. As a Victim, he felt justified to Bully me into making an exception for his wife.

The guilt trip (in these examples the implication is that I am not a good or generous person unless I do it his way, and with his way, whoever is disempowered gets the help they need) is meant to evoke an emotional response from the other. Any emotional response, whether it is submitting to the guilt or angrily pushing the guilt trip away, only continues the Drama. By not responding emotionally, the trip can be defused. If I had responded in anger, I would have taken up the Bully position and my former client would have felt further Victimized. If I had responded apologetically, I would have invited more attack from my former client. Instead, what I did was respond that this was nothing personal and that all clients are subject to the same rules regarding cancellations and rescheduling. He could accept that or not. Offering a choice in a self-assertive way tends to defuse these types of situations because it puts everyone back in a position of power.

It could have been that my former client would have still taken my response personally, but instead he did not. However, I did make it plain that if his wife had more sessions with me she was the one who had to do all the communicating with me about her sessions. Neither of them understood this boundary, and needless to say, neither of them worked with me again. The best response when finding yourself on the Drama Triangle is to not engage it. If you do discover that one person is stuck in Rescuer it is likely that that person will have hidden and unspoken expectations of future behavior once the first "favor" is offered. In some cases it is a healthy choice not to interact with that person. In other cases it might be fine to interact on a very limited basis with clear expectations on behavior.

If you saw yourself as the Guilt Tripping Rescuer in this example, the way out of this pattern of behavior is to examine your assumptions about how you interact with others. Do you have a hidden agenda? Do you expect special treatment because of favors you have done for the other? Do you allow the relationship to progress with no strings attached? Are you denying the other person their power? Do people disappoint you by not responding in the generous way that you believe you treat others? If so, it is likely that you are a Rescuer with a hidden agenda of granting favors in exchange for special treatment in the future. The practice for the Rescuer is to give back power and to keep exchanges energetically equal in the present. What this means is letting each exchange be complete and in the moment so that no cords remain attached. It also means treating yourself with respect—setting limits with how much you give to others, because if the Rescuer over-gives, she naturally sets up an imbalance, and then resentment and disappointment can follow. Once the Rescuer treats herself with respect, then respect for others and their personal power also follows.

6 THE EMPATH AS COLLUDING RESCUER

Perhaps the most troublesome trap an Empath can fall into is Collusion with whatever Story is unfolding around her. Empaths, because of childhood training, easily take on the agendas of other people and groups of people. Although the Empath may do this to please others, many times the Empath unconsciously tunes into and plays out the parts for other people's dramas without being aware that that is what she is doing, even when those parts cast her into a villain role or a painful role. Empaths commonly fall into the trap of Colluding as a Rescuer in someone else's Drama. Usually the person instigating the Drama is in the Victim position and has an unhealed mother-wound. This person looks for someone to be the mother-substitute, and Empaths tend to fall into that Rescuer role.

People who are invested in the Rescuer Role are horrified to hear that being a Rescuer means taking power from another person. The Rescuer takes responsibility for the life of a Victim and in effect tries to fix the Victim. Empaths in particular hold the emotional wellbeing of the Victim in their hands without even knowing that this type of Victim deliberately gives the Rescuer power. The Victim may willingly transfer power to the Rescuer and may like being Rescued. In extremely unhealthy cases, the Rescuer makes a grab for power, overriding the Victim's sovereignty when no Rescue was requested. This can be a disturbing realization for a Rescuer who thinks he is in that position only to do good in the world, or to be helpful, or to be a healer. But too much help can make the Victim even more helpless than before help was offered.

Part of what makes noticing the Rescuer role hard is that the group dynamic in place during childhood reinforces Rescuer behavior by demanding, expecting, or rewarding it, and punishing the failed Rescuer when that behavior is not in evidence. The Rescuer most times is on automatic pilot, Rescuing without realizing that is what he is doing. The key for a Rescuer in getting off the Drama Triangle is to remember that the only person he can change is himself. He has control of his own thoughts, feelings, and behaviors. Anyone else's is out of bounds. Trying to change another's behavior, thoughts, or feelings is the definition of controlling others.

Many Empaths are susceptible to Rescuing because of the belief that they must manage the crazy making behavior of others within her original family; that unconscious belief leads to the same pattern manifesting with others who need extra emotional support. The clue Empaths should look for is if she puts more energy into the relationship than others do, and if that energy is reciprocated. Usually a Victim puts less energy into the relationship and cannot offer the same support as a Rescuer Empath. If the family system or the community is unhealthy, the entire community will also expect the Rescuer Role from the Empath, and may even depend on the Empath to keep the Victim from getting into too much trouble, or expect the Empath to make heavy allowances for inappropriate and hurtful behavior from the Victim. The Empath, if she isn't careful, can come to believe in her Role and will then Collude not just with the Victim, but also with the entire family or community.

In my practice, I commonly have Empath clients with mothers who needed Rescuing. These Empaths have literally been trained to be of service to their mothers—the relationship has been flipped upside down. The Empath grows up seeing a weak mother, or seeing her mother unable to keep up a strong front without her support. While in a healthy child-mother relationship, the child is expected to grow up and leave the mother, these Empaths feel guilt for following the pull of adulthood. Even though the Empath may know that she needs to step out of the role and move on with her own life, the Guilt at abandoning her mother is so excruciating, it takes several attempts to break out of the role and change the relationship. On top of this, these unhealthy mothers usually punish their daughters for leaving.

Rescuers tend to think that it is their fault when someone they care about feels badly. Not only do Rescuers feel responsible for the feelings of others, they also feel responsible for changing those feelings. And the people who want to be Rescued may feel that the Rescuer ought to do something differently. This sets up tremendous Guilt within the Rescuer for the failed Rescuing. Extremely unhealthy examples of this are the battered spouse who feels so much guilt she cannot leave the abusive husband because **he** will feel abandoned. People who Rescue are easily Guilt tripped by others, especially when trying to relinquish their position as Rescuer. The belief to be shed goes something like, "I, and I alone, am responsible for this marriage, this relationship, this family, etc." Once responsibility is meted out equally, freedom from Drama for the Rescuer can begin.

Giving up the Rescuer role comes when we understand the cost of being in the Rescuer position. While an Empath may gain a special place with this person, or with the group, Rescuing tends to be draining, and also sets the Empath up later to be Bullied (Victimized). Empaths then tend to be confused about what went wrong, and they may desperately want to fix it. But Drama can never be fixed, and Victims must learn to fix themselves by stepping off the Drama Triangle. Rescuer Empaths literally cannot fix it because the Victim and situation is not hers to fix. The Family or group may shift that responsibility to the Empath, and the Empath may feel responsible for fixing the Victim, but eventually the emotional health of the Empath and the ability to be herself comes in jeopardy. The Empath is put in an untenable position. The only way out is to leave the Drama Triangle all together and stop Colluding with the Family or group. However, pressure from the Family System to continue to Collude must be expected. The Empath must stand firm even when the alternating intense feelings of guilt, anger, and fear arise she tries to break out of the habit of Colluding. (The Victim tends to feel fear, the Resucer, guilt, and the Bully, anger. As we leave the Drama Triangle, we tend to alternate amongst these feelings until we are clear. See the Guilt, Anger, and Fear Cycle essay in the Family System Ebook for more details.)

The pressure from the Group or Family can easily overtake an Empath, and sometimes the Empath deliberately falls back into role playing as a way of not exploring her own power, independence, and individuality. However, once the Empath gives up Colluding with a particular person, there is really no comfortable way of going back. Colluding is never satisfactory afterwards, and never again feels real. The Illusion is now seen for what it is, even though others may be happy to live in the Illusion. If the Empath chooses to stay anyway, she is likely to move from Rescuer to Bully and take revenge or treat the people within the dynamic cruelly, thus perpetuating the Drama and wasting her time and energy.

When the Empath gives up Colluding, she is free to do whatever she wants with her life. This can be shocking for the Empath. Suddenly she has so much time, space and energy when she stops playing in someone else's Drama. The Empath stepping away from Drama and the Rescuer role is stepping toward personal empowerment and enjoyment of her own creativity. While this outcome may sound wonderful, for many Empaths having this freedom is scarier than engaging in Dramas. It is here that diving into personal work, especially around the Empath's Soul's Purpose in life can be very helpful. Empaths are meant to enjoy life, be creative, and serve in the world. It will not happen through Drama and the Rescuer Role.

7 THE OVER-EDUCATED RIGHTEOUS BULLY

The Over-Educated Righteous Bully has had a wounding, usually by a parent, which is so deep the Bully may embark on a lifelong path of punishing all those who remind her of that parent. This person relives the original wounding/s by drawing in others and then lashing out at them for all their faults and their betrayals. The person who is attacked is the representative for the bad parent, so these attacks are even more vicious because the Bully gets to attack the parent and say all the things that she would not dare say to the parent lest she lose any scrap of love and approval she might have.

The Righteous Bully usually can be spotted by the string of broken relationships left in her wake. These can be both primary relationships and friendships. The Righteous Bully lives on the drama triangle and plays all roles well. But, the best payoff for her is to be Bully. (This Bully can be described as the Type Eight, or the Get-Things-Done-Guy, on the Enneagram; however other types can play this Bully as well.) To get there, she usually takes up the Rescuer position and pulls in someone who isn't empowered. These are great people for the Bully to choose because then she can pick them apart later when she moves to Bully.

The Righteous Bully works hard to save her friend or her lover. And then she becomes disillusioned with them because they are either weak or they do not improve themselves. She becomes mean. Because the other is fairly disempowered, they may be afraid of the Bully and not speak up on time, or just become passive as a way of checking out and protecting themselves. These people wait for the

Bully to reject them, and then move on with their lives.

When the Bully rejects them, she momentarily feels great satisfaction, but later, if she runs into them again, or hears of them again, she sees that they have moved on, and that makes her feel even more Victimized. They didn't need her after all, and she feels the old wounding of not being included in her original family. She has moved successfully all the way around the Drama Triangle yet again. Each time she violently rejects one of these people, she cannot forget them. Her feelings of anger and bitterness follow her, years after she rejected them as unworthy of her association. She becomes frustrated and disgusted and can't understand why these unworthy people get what they want, when she does not. She remains either alone and dissatisfied, or with someone and disgusted.

The disillusionment can lead the Righteous Bully to seek professional help. With most Bullies, Bullying is the preferred way to defend the self from feeling the pain of being weak and worthless as is. This type of Bully is usually very good at learning all the self-empowering tools and studying up on all the self-healing she can. She becomes very knowledgeable to the point of knowing every modality and its jargon. However, there is a defensiveness to gathering all this knowledge; for the Bully it is weaponry to use later against her new parent stand in, the incompetent healer. But because she is still operating from Bully, she usually picks healers that are beginners that she senses she can easily Bully later.

I had the interesting experience of working with a Righteous Bully. This woman knew she was a Bully and she didn't like her behavior, but it brought her all sorts of success with her career. She was an expert at getting things done, and was well rewarded for this. But, it didn't serve her in her relationships. She wanted a softer side to herself so she could be more feminine and perhaps attract a new mate into her life.

What was interesting about this woman was that because she was so driven to heal herself, she tried to make it happen without thinking about the boundaries of her healing assistants. I saw this woman run over several healers to the point where they were not interested in working with her any longer, but she was so aggressive they became afraid of asserting themselves with her. Most of them waited passively until she became disillusioned with their work and went away.

When she worked with me, even though I explained that it was not a good idea to have shamanic work done more than once or twice a month, she could not hear the boundary I was setting with her, and worked with other healers behind my back. Her emotional overwhelm from those other sessions was something that I ended up fielding, even though I had thought we had agreed she would abide by my guidelines. When I found out, I should have chosen to not continue working with her. However, I was fooled by her willingness to heal, her apologies, and her promises to slow down.

Her brazenness in ignoring instructions and boundaries was part of her strategy in getting things done and getting what she wanted. What was ironic was it was this very behavior of controlling—if she just had enough soul retrievals she would get what she wanted—was what needed to be given up. What this behavior stated was that she didn't trust Spirit to partner with her; she had to do it all herself. She didn't trust others to work with her freely and honestly; they were either all incompetent or too slow for her. She was special. She could ignore the rules.

After seeing and hearing how her other relationships with healers had gone, I found myself in the position of knowing that I was next in line to be attacked. This had nothing to do with me—I was simply the stand in for the original parent figure that had failed her. And sure enough, that attack eventually came, including complaints about my work to other colleagues, mentors, and teachers. Of course, my teachers weren't fooled by her behavior, and I was relieved that her Drama had finally played itself out. She could move on to the next incompetent healer.

The Righteous Bully is firmly entrenched in not taking responsibility for her anger and bitterness because whoever has wronged her is responsible for her bitterness. Focusing on that person's incompetence becomes the distraction from true self-mastery. From the outside these Bullies look highly competent and intelligent, so this simply reinforces their unconsciousness around their Victim position. To them, Victims are weak, and they are the direct opposite. So, it is difficult for them to see how they play out the Drama Triangle.

In order for these people to heal, they have to come in contact with how weak and powerless they are. Most of them cannot do it; it is simply too painful and their strategy of being a Bully is too successful in the world despite their failed relationships. If you are in relationship with a Righteous Bully, it is pretty likely that once the rescuing behavior is done, the Bully is going to become disillusioned with you, and then the attacks will begin. The best outcome is to be put on the bone pile with all the others and then move on with your life.

If you have become embittered by your past relationships, if you are angry at others who have what they want and do not deserve it, if you see most healers as incompetent and unable to help you, and if you are seen as being highly competent but intimidating, you are probably an Over-Educated Righteous Bully, especially if you take actions in the outside world to punish those who have betrayed you or hurt you with their incompetence. To liberate yourself from this persona, the defensive mechanism of competence and control must be given up, at least for a moment, in order to dive in and explore the weakness, cowardliness, and pain that lurks beneath. Strength for the Righteous Bully is a defense against vulnerability and the pain of not being good enough as is. Knowing it all and being right for the Righteous Bully is a defense against the discomfort of uncertainty.

Because co-creating with Spirit always means living on the edge of uncertainty, Righteous Bullies are easily spotted in the Spiritual Seeking Community. All the knowledge they have gained has a hollow ring to it, because others sense that the Bully can talk, but does not walk. Isolation for them at this point can become even more painful. However, for the Righteous Bully, it is the perfect opportunity to dive in and heal themselves. The key is to remember that at the core, all needs to lash out at others stem from the need to punish the incompetent, undeserving parent figure or figures. Until the Righteous Bully can understand this and choose not to act on such impulses, they remain stuck.

The irony is that once the Righteous Bully allows that they are mean-spirited because they are trying to protect themselves from feeling weak, they are able to have more compassion for themselves. They begin to love themselves the way they wished others did. Once they give themselves that love, then the defensiveness begins to give way to compassion and understanding for others. They are still competent in the world, but the focus on the incompetence of others diminishes, and they are able to finally create the relationships they want. And others are now able to relate to them without an underlying sense of fear of the next attack.

8 THE OVERWHELMED EMPATH AS BULLY

One Empath pitfall that can be very difficult for the Empath to see and master is curbing psychic and verbal attack against others who have unintentionally overwhelmed the Empath's sensitivity. The Empath, being sensitive, many times cannot handle input that the non-Empath brings. The non-Empath usually does not find the input troublesome or upsetting. This feeling of overwhelm can cause the Empath to blame the other for overwhelming her, when that person intended no harm.

Even if the Empath understands that no harm was intended, the Empath can be so overwhelmed, and her emotional state can be so stirred up that she can unintentionally psychically attack the non-Empath by sending out attacking emotional energy, with the assumption that the other is to blame for her stirred up emotions. The non-Empath may not be as sensitive as her, but on some level feels the psychic attack. The Empath may even Bully the non-Empath verbally, accusing the other of an intended malicious attack.

The non-Empath then reacts negatively. A common conclusion that the non-Empath may draw is that the Empath's sensitivity is the problem, when in fact it is the psychic attack that is the problem. Then the Empath concludes that this person cannot honor her sensitivity, not realizing that it was her own original psychic attack that invited the non-Empath's response. Or, the non-Empath may decide that the Empath is oversensitive and unreasonable, and may leave or may limit the relationship, reinforcing the Empath's core wounds of abandonment and of rejection and the belief that she is not accepted for her Empathy.

The sending of negative emotional energy laced with Blame toward another is a form of psychic attack. Learning not to send Blame towards others is an aspect of the Empath's Shadow Work, which will be discussed further in the next Ebook. The beginning of mastery of this pitfall comes with accepting that emotional energy must be scrupulously watched. No one, not even Empaths who have been wronged, have the right to spread anger, fear, chaos, or overwhelm to others. And those others are not to blame and are not responsible for creating that emotional state within us. The truth is that we must learn to deal with our emotional state and to be responsible for that state at all times.

We must accept that we are more likely to be overwhelmed and over-stimulated by input that does not overwhelm others. When we are in the overwhelm state, we are likely to react poorly. It is during those times that we must take steps not to exacerbate our situation by sending irritation and blame toward others. Ironically, when the Empath does make the mistake of sending out negative emotional energy, it is usually more destructive for her than what was sent to her in the first place because she feels not only her own overwhelm but the other person's negative reaction and anger.

If the non-Empath feels attacked without cause, it makes it very likely that the Empath will find no sympathy for her distressed state. In fact, the non-Empath, if he is not in control of his emotions, is likely to respond with an attack of his own, thus perpetuating Drama when none was intended by anyone. If the Empath is married to a Get Things Done Guy (a type 8 on the Enneagram), the Drama is likely to escalate to proportions that crush the Empath. If the Empath is married to a Peacemaker (a Type 9 on the Enneagram), the Drama will escalate in the form of passive aggression and sarcasm. If the Empath is married to a Giving Persona, a Hero, or a Logical Scientist the Empath will be seen as the over-emotional and unreasonable one and become the scapegoat. If the Empath is married to another Empath, the Drama may escalate into a contest of who is the most victimized and wronged.

So, how does the Empath handle these situations? The Empath has a tendency to respond to everything that comes her way. Instead we must practice observing our own reactions. If our emotions are stirred up, we should probably wait before issuing declarations or ultimatums. But another option that many Empaths fail to consider is one of not responding at all. As Empaths we may feel the urge to set boundaries and limits and tell the other not to do it again, or worse, we may feel the urge to "educate" the non-Empath on what he has done wrong and how he needs to change his behavior. When we become overwhelmed by a stressful situation, we must pause before we react. We need to slow down our reactions before moving forward to state boundaries and set limits with others because if we are feeling Victimized when we do so, we are likely to come across as Bullies, unintentionally creating Drama. It is fine to have that conversation once our emotional state is calmer and we're not throwing our emotional energy around in the form of blame, but we must ask ourselves, is it necessary? Is this a good use of my energy? Perhaps the transgression can pass without having to respond to it if no harm was intended, and especially if Drama would be stirred up by our speaking up.

We must realize that the rest of the world simply is not as sensitive as we are. And while we must take care of ourselves, we must be careful to stay out of Drama when we are feeling overwhelmed. (In another eBook, we will go over when to speak up and set limits without Drama.) Practice non-engagement instead. Practice leaving the room or waiting an hour or a day before responding to something that has upset us. Take the time to see what the other person's perspective could be. Was it intended to upset us? Is it likely to occur again? Are we upset enough that we cannot respond without blame? Slowing down our reactions is a great skill to master for the Empath. Not only does it help keep us out of unnecessary and unintended Dramas, but it makes us less likely to be run solely by our emotional state.

9 CREATING SAFE CONTAINERS FOR YOUR FAMILY—LIVING DRAMA FREE

One of the more common relationship issues I have seen my clients deal with is around priority. When one spouse complains that the other is not making her the priority in their lives, I look closely to see if two relationship keystones are in place. The first is the creation of good boundaries, which naturally help organize priorities, and the second is to make sure that the spouse with the apparent priority issue is not stuck in the Victim position on the Drama Triangle. This second issue may seem odd and unrelated, but most of the time, when couples are fighting, the Drama Triangle is at work.

When we create safe boundaries within our family, we are stating to each other where each person stands in the relationship. Each person naturally knows what to expect from the other, and communication usually flows well, or can be improved with knowledge of how each person likes to communicate. (Is she a feeler, a thinker, a doer, etc.) The boundaries around the couple allow each person to feel safe in the relationship. Each person knows that other people on the outside will not intrude unexpectedly. The wife knows that the husband is the buffer between her and his relationships with the outside world and visa versa.

When we have good boundaries, each person knows that he can count on the other to set limits with the outside world. These limits and spoken and unspoken expectations form a container around the couple. As the couple honors those limits and boundaries, a feeling of safety fills their container. Falling into the Victim position always upsets the safety of the container because the Victim is powerless. When we are disempowered we can no longer effectively set limits, and then encroachment from the outside and even the inside begins. Usually the Victim position is taken up unconsciously and neither partner is fully aware of what has happened.

When one person falls into the Victim position, they naturally pull either a Bully or a Rescuer out of their spouse. Suddenly the spouse can find herself trying to solve all the problems in the relationship by herself. Or, she turns into a nitpicking nag. Or she alternates between Rescuing and Bullying. Or, she is neither, but the person playing Victim perceives her as a Bully. This can be incredibly frustrating and confusing for both people. Without knowing what has happened, the behavior can escalate and previously loving couples can find themselves in a vicious cycle where one person is demanding the other set limits but demands it in a bullying way, and the other feels put upon and victimized by both the spouse and the outside world. Eventually both people feel victimized and stuck.

The way out of the Drama is for at least one person in the couple to step out of playing any of the three roles. I had a client who came from a very close-knit family where involvement and closeness was expected from all members, including spouses. When my client married, his wife was not used to such closeness, and eventually wanted more distance from his family members, including the option of not participating in every family event. My client at first did not want to allow his wife to have this distance; from his perspective she knew what she was getting into when she married him. The wife insisted on her space, to which my client agreed, but he continued his closeness with his family.

At first, this agreement seemed to go well, but then when his wife became sick, my client, instead of taking care of his wife, honored commitments to other family members instead. Understandably, his wife felt like she wasn't the priority in his life, his family was. Enough of these incidents led to the wife feeling much resentment toward her husband, and to demanding that he put their marriage first, or else she would conclude that they didn't have the marriage that she wanted. Her argument was that his behavior was evidence that she could not count on him in the future, that what she could count on was his not being there when she needed his support.

My client found himself in a double bind. He wanted happiness for himself, his family members, and his wife, but found that he could no longer make everyone happy at the same time. From that position, he felt powerless to change the situation for the better. From his perspective his wife was not supporting him in what was important to him: maintaining close connection with his family members and honoring their requests and unconscious expectations for his time and energy.

My client felt pulled in two directions at once and was unable to take action. His paralysis seemed to aggravate his wife even more than his going to family events. As his inaction continued, the wife became more and more angry. From his perspective, he was hostage to his wife's hostility. He began doing what he could to avoid arguments with her, but this strategy escalated the tension between them. On top of this his family members decided that his wife was the problem and they wanted my client to make her be reasonable or to leave her so he could be happy. Now from his perspective his family, whom he had been giving all this support at the expense of his marriage, were coming down on him during a time when *he* needed understanding and support.

What my client had trouble seeing is that he had fallen into the Victim position. From that helpless state, he had turned his wife into a Bully, and his family into another Bully. His family was trying to Rescue him by telling him to leave his Bullying wife. My client began to see his wife as to blame, by asking him to change his family dynamic over which he had no control. From his perspective he was powerless and had only choices that led to his unhappiness. If he did what his wife wanted, his family would be unhappy, if he did what his family wanted, then his wife would be unhappy.

When he was able to see that his powerlessness was absolving him of responsibility of taking action, in other words, that he was behaving as a Victim, he was horrified. But, taking action was still very hard for him. Avoiding conflict and making everyone happy had ironically led to more conflict and more unhappiness. When he understood that he had to set limits with both his wife and his family by making choices for just himself, he recreated a safe container for himself and he stepped out of the Victim role.

Because his family members turned out not to offer the support he thought they would and he realized that they also took for granted his support, he wanted to change those relationships so they were more equal in reciprocation. He set limits with his family by not being as available to them as he had been when he was single. His family members, still viewing him as a Victim, interpreted this as his wife's controlling him and as his bowing to her demands, but he held firm and had no regrets. In fact, he was angry with them for not adjusting, but he was careful not to perceive them as Bullies and fall back into the Victim position.

Part of making sure that he didn't fall into Drama was releasing his attachment to how he thought they should behave. While he had a distinct opinion about their behavior toward his wife, he was careful to catch himself thinking that they should behave differently. He had to come to accept that they were the way they were, without expecting them to change. Once he was able to do this, it was easier not to fall back into the Victim position and blame them for his discomfort at changing his relationship with them.

Then he took a look at his relationship with his wife. From an empowered position he was able to see that his wife had been asking him to create a safe container for their marriage, not dump his family members all together. He realized that by not having good boundaries with his family he was inadvertently leaving a hole in their marriage container and leaving her feeling insecure and unsafe. Although in his mind before he had always thought his relationship with his wife was his first priority, he saw that he needed to put their commitments and needs ahead of others with actions and with a clear internal motivation. Ultimately he decided that this would add to his happiness, and that he was doing it not because his wife told him to, but because he was making the active choice himself. At first his wife questioned his motivations; she did not want him to act just to please her. It took some time for her to trust that he was acting from his center rather than trying to keep the peace with her. Eventually she did trust him, and she was not threatened when later he began renegotiating relationship with his original family members who were willing to adjust to his new limits.

My client had the shocking realization of what it means to be in the Role of the Family Rescuer—family members tended to have the expectation that he would take care of their needs ahead of his own and even ahead of his new family's needs. In fact, he was obligated to do so. Giving up this role within his family meant upsetting the Family dynamic temporarily until a new equilibrium could be reached. My client was angry to discover himself in such a position, but he also had to give up the perks of being the Family Rescuer—he was no longer seen as the reliable, self-sacrificing one.

The issue intruding on the couple's container isn't always just extended family. In fact, in this client's case, he also had to look at the way he held his career, and the way he held long-term friendships. He had been single up into his mid-thirties, and had not anticipated the space in the form of attention and time that his marriage needed. In the case of work, his wife did not like the long hours he was putting in. But, learning from the experience with his extended family, instead of saying that he had to work long hours because that was what was expected (i.e. his boss was making him), he set the limit with his wife and said instead that he was choosing to work long hours.

His wife was unhappy with this, but was able to then ask if this was a temporary arrangement, or if this was a lifestyle. He was able to say that it was temporary, and that he was looking forward to the time they could spend more time together. He was surprised when his wife did not become angry but supported him by taking over more household duties to make his life easier. His wife had heard his limits and decided to adjust. Even if he had decided that he wanted to work longer hours than his wife preferred, stating this as his choice leaves his wife to choose what she wants. It could be that she'd choose to live with his longer work hours, or it could be that she'd choose not to. The important point is that each person remains empowered to make choices for themselves and the marriage. From knowing each other's limits and boundaries, we create clear expectations, a sense of safety, and containment for the relationship, and we also can interact in our relationships without falling into Drama.

10 CONCLUSION

As we move forward describing friendships and family dynamics in future eBooks, we'll naturally cover more example of the Drama Triangle. Until then, please use these examples to practice staying out of Drama. Remember, we Empaths tend to be hard on ourselves—if you catch yourself in a Drama, exit as gracefully as you can but offer yourself compassion. Drama is a collective phenomenon; every person has been caught on the Drama Triangle. Our task is to create a new collective phenomenon—as many people as possible free the Drama Triangle of Disempowerment.

11 RESOURCES

Here's a short list of my favorite books that got me started on my path:

Shamanism and Healing Work:
Shaman Healer Sage by Alberto Villoldo
Mending the Past Healing the Future with Soul Retrieval by Alberto Villoldo
The Reluctant Shaman by Kay Cordell Whitaker
Soul Retrieval by Sandra Ingerman

Intuition, the Chakra System and Psychic Development:
The Psychic Pathway by Sonia Choquette
True Balance by Sonia Choquette

Personal Transformation and Manifestation:
Your Heart's Desire by Sonia Choquette
Finding Your North Star by Martha Beck
Steering by Starlight by Martha Beck

The Spiritual Enneagram:
Personality Types by Don Richard Riso with Russ Hudson
Wisdom of the Enneagram by Don Riso and Russ Husdon

Creativity:
The Artist's Way by Julia Cameron

Vein of Gold by Julia Cameron

The following are teachers and schools that I highly recommend:

Sonia Choquette offers trainings and workshops for developing intuition.
Marv Harwood of Kimmapii Spirit Energies is the shaman I go to for graduate training
The Four Winds Society trains students to be shaman healers
Wake and Kinlen Wheeler of Sacred Pathways offer training and shaman gatherings

Contact Information:
If you would like to contact me, please visit my website at
www.elainelajoie.com My website has many free resources and essays for Empaths, plus a list of practicing shaman I highly recommend.
Much love to you,
Elaine

ABOUT THE AUTHOR

Elaine La Joie is a shaman and certified life coach. She has been in private practice since 2002 helping Empaths heal old traumas and patterns so that they can create the lives and relationships that they really want.

Before Elaine opened her practice she worked at the University of Texas Austin in the psychology department and at the Oregon Medical Laser Center as a researcher. Elaine holds degrees in physics and applied physics. She realized a few years into this career path that she was jealous of the other researchers who loved their careers. This, plus a psychic opening led her in a completely new and unexpected direction.

Not wanting to advertise as a psychic, Elaine went into Life Coaching instead. She trained with Coach For Life, became certified, and then was horrified when all her clients started asking for readings or training. After a few more years of resistance Elaine trained with the Four Winds Society and later with Marv Harwood of Alberta Canada.

Elaine maintains a limited private practice so she can concentrate on writing. She lives in Oregon with her family.

CPSIA information can be obtained
at www.ICGtesting.com
Printed in the USA
LVOW13s0021040717
540275LV00006B/110/P